This Doodle By Number
Belongs To

....

By Doodle Lovely

Your calm mind is the ultimate weapon against your challenges.

BRYANT MCGILL

WOOF!

Or, as we non-canine critters would say, 'HELLO!'

Doodle By Number™ isn't just for kids, it's for anyone who wants to quiet their busy thoughts, awaken their creative spirit, and enjoy the peace that comes with a little mindfulness.

And who better to guide us through a mindful activity than the master of mindfulness, our furry friend, the dog.

Dogs are pros at living in the moment, of experiencing the joy of small pleasures, and for their love of play.

That's why I designed this book: dogs and doodling are a natural fit, and we could all benefit from more of both.

You don't need to be an artist or an expert to enjoy doodling. You just need to start moving your pen across the paper, ready to follow the journey wherever it may lead.

Wishing you a tail-wagging day of doodles,

Melissa x

WHY DOODLE?

It's true! People have been doodling for millennia.
"Spontaneous drawing" has been studied and verified as a means
to decrease stress in our lives.

Taking pen in hand and using the rhythmic motions of doodling activates
the relaxation response within the brain. Just the thing to calm the chaos!

Playfulness
Doodling promotes
wellbeing, allowing you to
lighten your mood whenever
you feel overwhelmed.

Creative Freedom
Doodling is a workout
for the mind that can help
you focus on new ideas and
bring fresh insights.

Improved Focus
Doodling is a simple and
effective way to help you
concentrate and process
information.

DISCOVER
THE BENEFITS
OF DOODLING
TODAY

Manage Emotions
Doodling is a safe method
to evaluate unsettling
emotions, converting jumbled
feelings into a peaceful
state of mind.

Greater Productivity
Doodling can refresh your
mind and reset your thoughts,
allowing for a greater
sense of clarity.

Increased Memory
Studies indicate that while
listening to others, the brain
can recall 29% more
information while doodling.

How to use your

DOODLE *by* NUMBER™

Pick up a pen, your favorite marker, or pencil of any color.

At the bottom of each example page there is a selection
of five doodle patterns to choose from. Each pattern is
circled and numbered.

Follow the numbers to create a doodle pattern on the
opposite page. If you want to use more or less doodles, go for it!

Complete the *Doodle By Number™* and touch it up
to your satisfaction.

Feel free to make the doodle your own with your favorite
shapes, lines and patterns. Even add color if you like. Doodle-riffic!

Follow the numbers to match your doodles on the opposite page.

1 - Swirls   2 - Triangles   3 - Lines   4 - X's   5 - Dots

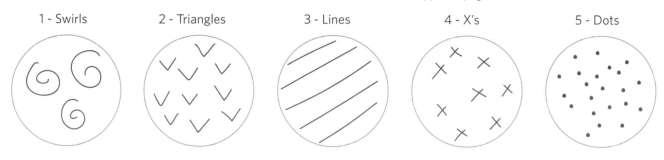

Love is a
four-legged
word.

UNKNOWN

Follow the numbers to match your doodles on the opposite page.

1 - Starbursts   2 - Triangles   3 - Loops   4 - Dashes   5 - Leaves

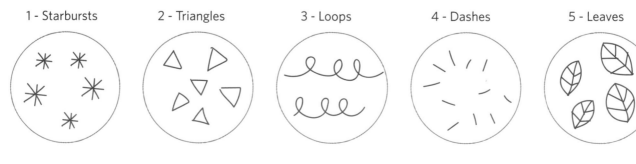

Such short little lives our pets have to spend with us, and they spend most of it waiting for us to come home each day.

JOHN GROGAN

Follow the numbers to match your doodles on the opposite page.

1 - Triple Lines

2 - Swirls

3 - Scallops

4 - Lines

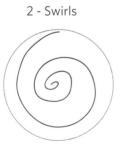

5 - X's

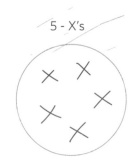

Self confidence is
the best outfit.
Own it and rock it!

UNKNOWN

Follow the numbers to match your doodles on the opposite page.

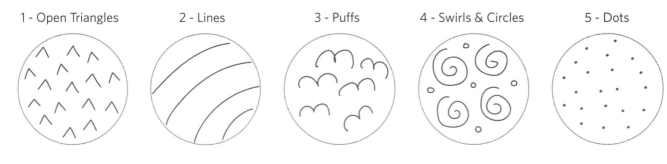

1 - Open Triangles   2 - Lines   3 - Puffs   4 - Swirls & Circles   5 - Dots

No one appreciates the
very special genius of
your conversation
as a dog does.

CHRISTOPHER MORLEY

Follow the numbers to match your doodles on the opposite page.

| 1 - Double U's | 2 - Loops | 3 - Circle Pods | 4 - Lines | 5 - Swirls |

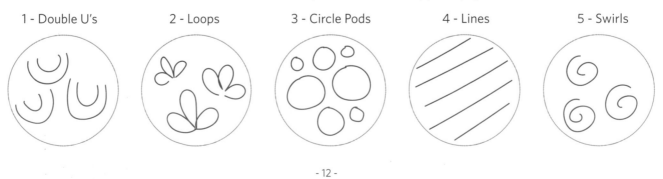

Believe in
yourself and you will
be unstoppable!

EMILY GUAY

Follow the numbers to match your doodles on the opposite page.

1 - X's   2 - Starbursts   3 - Open Squares   4 - Puffs   5 - Lines

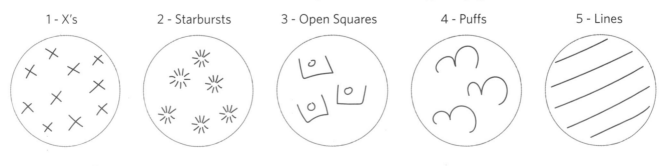

You are never too old to learn something new,
or too young to learn too much.

SUZY KASSEM

Follow the numbers to match your doodles on the opposite page.

1 - Wavy Lines   2 - Circles   3 - Triangles   4 - Arches   5 - Zig Zags

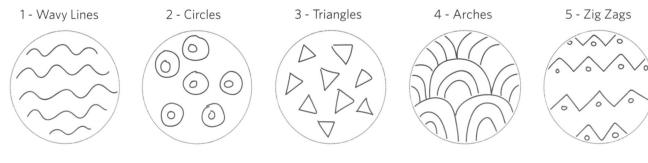

There's a saying. If you want someone to love you forever, buy a dog, feed it and keep it around.

DICK DALE

Follow the numbers to match your doodles on the opposite page.

1 - Triple Lines   2 - X's   3 - Divided Circles   4 - Lines   5 - Loops

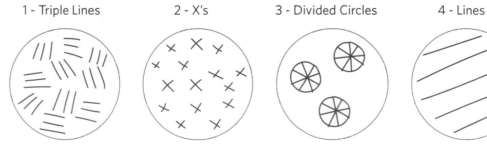

Happiness is a warm puppy.

CHARLES SHULTZ

Follow the numbers to match your doodles on the opposite page.

1 - Arches	2 - Circles	3 - Triangles	4 - 7's	5 - Lines

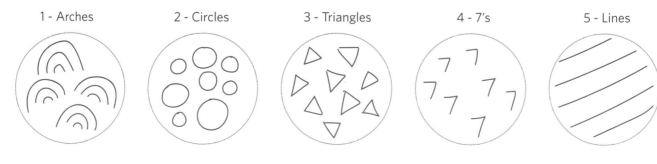

Bliss is the result of a silent conversation between me and my dog.

UNKNOWN

Follow the numbers to match your doodles on the opposite page.

1 - Lines	2 - Open Triangles	3 - Zig Zags Circles	4 - Triple Lines	5 - X's

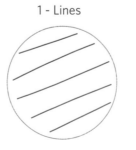 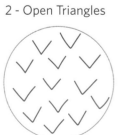   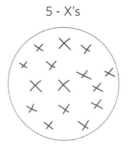

No matter how little money
and how few possessions you own,
having a dog makes you rich.

LOUIS SABIN

Follow the numbers to match your doodles on the opposite page.

1 - Line Patterns	2 - Arches	3 - W's	4 - Dashes	5 - Swirls

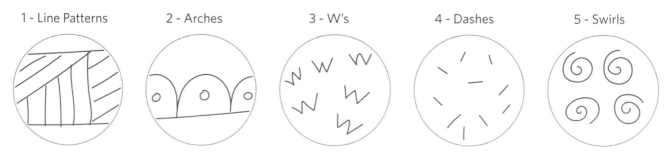

The journey of life is sweeter
when traveled with a dog.

BRIDGET WILLOUGHBY

WOOF

Follow the numbers to match your doodles on the opposite page.

1 - Triangles   2 - Arches   3 - Z's   4 - Starbursts   5 - Scallops

What do dogs do on their day off?
Can't lie around, that's their job.

GEORGE CARLIN

Follow the numbers to match your doodles on the opposite page.

| 1 - Line Patterns | 2 - X's | 3 - Wavy Lines | 4 - Circles | 5 - Leaves |

Just enjoy
where you
are now.

UNKNOWN

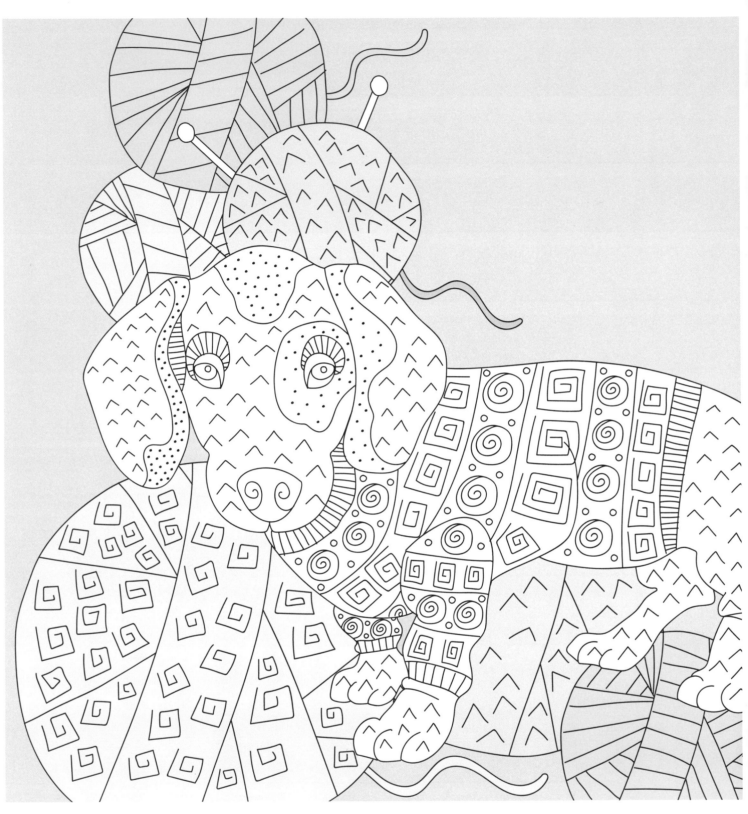

Follow the numbers to match your doodles on the opposite page.

1 - Open Triangles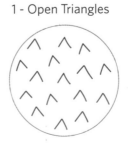

2 - Lines

3 - Square Swirls

4 - Swirl Patterns

5 - Dots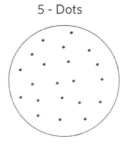

If you don't own a dog, at least one, there is not necessarily anything wrong with you, but there may be something wrong with your life.

ROGER A. CARAS

Follow the numbers to match your doodles on the opposite page.

1 - Triangles   2 - Stars   3 - Dashes   4 - Wavy Lines   5 - Circles

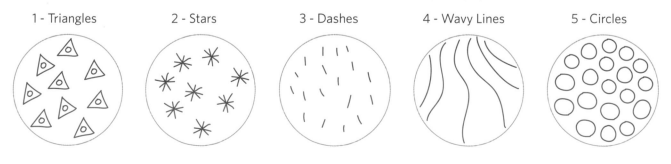

Never, ever underestimate the importance of having fun.

RANDY PAUSCH

Follow the numbers to match your doodles on the opposite page.

1 - Arches   2 - Zig Zag Lines   3 - Lines   4 - Dashes   5 - Circles

A dog is the only thing on earth that loves you more than you love yourself.

JOSH BILLINGS

Follow the numbers to match your doodles on the opposite page.

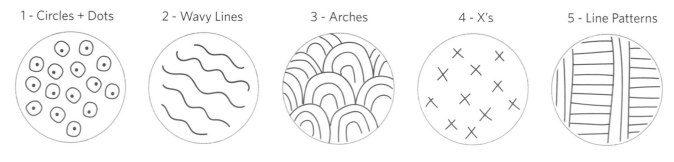

1 - Circles + Dots   2 - Wavy Lines   3 - Arches   4 - X's   5 - Line Patterns

My fashion philosophy is, if you're not covered in dog hair, your life is empty.

ELAYNE BOOSLERP

Follow the numbers to match your doodles on the opposite page.

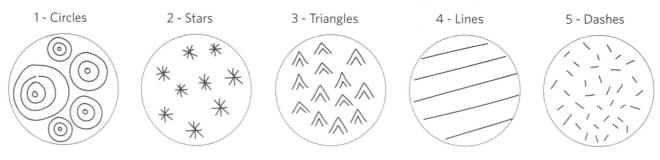

1 - Circles   2 - Stars   3 - Triangles   4 - Lines   5 - Dashes

*I just want to be in my sweats,
walk my dog, watch TV and eat pizza.*

AMERICA FERRERA

Follow the numbers to match your doodles on the opposite page.

1 - Cross Hatches   2 - Triangles   3 - Lines   4 - Wavy Lines   5 - Florals

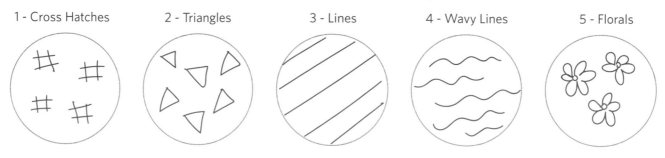

Live.
Laugh. Bark.

UNKNOWN

Follow the numbers to match your doodles on the opposite page.

1 - Open Squares   2 - Wavy Lines   3 - Arches   4 - Starbursts   5 - Loops

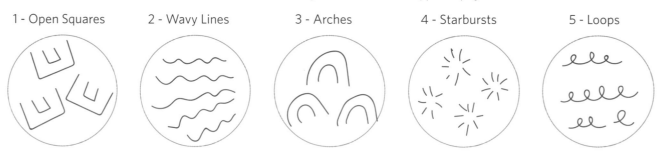

Retain a calm heart, sit like a turtle, walk swiftly like a pigeon, and sleep like a dog.

LI CHING-YUEN

Follow the numbers to match your doodles on the opposite page.

1 - Dash Pods   2 - Wavy Lines   3 - Arches   4 - Circles   5 - Lines

One way to get the most out of life is to look upon it as an adventure.

WILLIAM FEATHER JONATHAN SWIFT

Follow the numbers to match your doodles on the opposite page.

1 - Rain Drops   2 - Wavy Lines   3 - Dashes   4 - Arches   5 - Circle Pods

The trick is to enjoy life.
Don't wish away your days,
waiting for better ones ahead.

MARJORIE PAY HINCKLEY

Follow the numbers to match your doodles on the opposite page.

1 - Half Circles   2 - Puffs   3 - Scallop Patterns   4 - Lines   5 - Arches

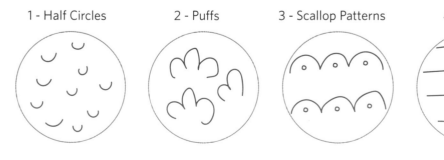
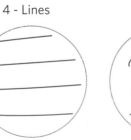

Dogs have boundless
enthusiasm but
no sense of shame.
I should have a dog
as a life coach.

MOBY

Follow the numbers to match your doodles on the opposite page.

1 - Woven Waves	2 - Swirls	3 - Wavy Lines	4 - Lines	5 - Puffs

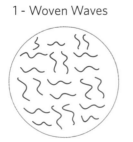  

I believe, everyday, you should have one exquisite moment.

AUDREY HEPBURN

Follow the numbers to match your doodles on the opposite page.

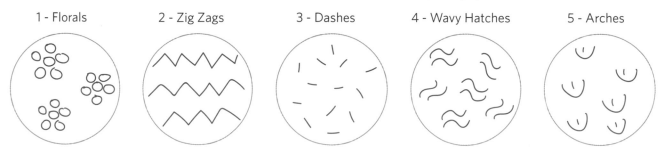

1 - Florals

2 - Zig Zags

3 - Dashes

4 - Wavy Hatches

5 - Arches

It's not the size of
the dog in the fight,
it's the size of the
fight in the dog.

MARK TWAIN

Follow the numbers to match your doodles on the opposite page.

1 - Puffs   2 - Arches   3 - Zig Zags   4 - Lines   5 - X's

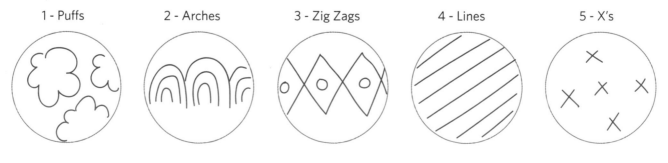

The best therapist
has four legs

UNKNOWN

Follow the numbers to match your doodles on the opposite page.

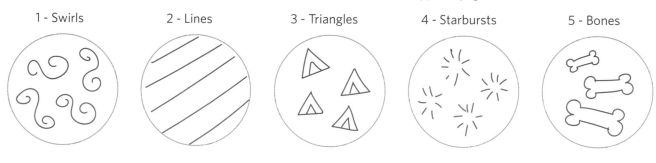

1 - Swirls   2 - Lines   3 - Triangles   4 - Starbursts   5 - Bones

Keep looking up.
That's the secret
of life.

SNOOPY

Follow the numbers to match your doodles on the opposite page.

1 - Square Swirls   2 - Circles   3 - W's   4 - Half Circles   5 - Lines

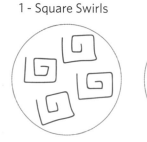 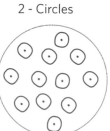   

Follow the numbers to match your doodles on the opposite page.

1 - Florals   2 - Cross Hatches   3 - Leaves   4 - Wavy Lines   5 - Swirls

Scratch a dog
and you'll find a
permanent job.

FRANKLIN P. JONES

Follow the numbers to match your doodles on the opposite page.

1 - Half Circles   2 - Wavy Lines   3 - Dashes   4 - Loop Pattern   5 - Swirls

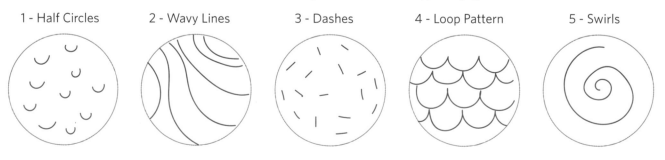

Life is too
important to
be taken
seriously.

OSCAR WILDE

Meet the Doodler

MELISSA LLOYD is an international doodler, designer, teacher, author and inspirationalist. Her passion for creativity can be found globally on products, environments and in the hearts of those with whom she has connected.

Melissa combines her twenty plus years of experience in professional design and communication with her passion and connection to humanity, psychology, art therapy and mindfulness; infusing a deep understanding of self.

Melissa teaches soul-care through creative practices and encourages you to learn how to navigate the stormy seas of life, reducing stress and rejuvenating your mind.

By honoring your creative soul and the celebration of living in the moment, Melissa inspires you to bring joy back into your life by finding a place of peace internally. Her transformational approach to creativity, through doodling and living, inspires others to live a healthier and happier life. 'Always Be You... For You.'

Melissa splits her time between mothering, creating, teaching and living in her little Cottage By The Sea. To discover more of Melissa's work visit: **DoodleLovely.com**

DOODLE *Lovely*™

A smile is the prettiest thing you can wear.

Did you enjoy this *Doodle By Number*™? We would love to hear your feedback!
Please email us: **hello@doodlelovely.com**

Connect with us to know when the next edition of *Doodle By Number*™
will be available in our online shop.
www.DoodleLovely.com